# BARCELONA
## A PICTORIAL BOOK OF GAUDÍ'S CITY

# 155 Colour illustrations

BONECHI

# CONTENTS

ISBN 88-7009-865-6

*Panorama of the city.*

# A BIT OF HISTORY

It was the Phoenicians and the Greeks who started Barcelona off as a trading center. But it was the Carthaginians who gave the city its name, «Barcino», in honor of Hannibal's father, Hamilcar Barca. Not long after the beginning of the Second Punic War (200 B.C.) Scipio's armies conquered the Carthaginian city. Barcino fell under Roman rule and as «Colonia Julia Augusta Pia Faventia» became a colony. Rome ruled for six centuries and not until the decline of the empire did the barbarian invasions begin. Barcelona was conquered by the Visigoths and the Vandals and was the temporary capital during the Visigothic reign of Ataulf. Even so it continued to be important from a religious point of view and the councils of 540 and 589 were held here. Spain was one of the areas where the Catholic and Muslim cultures clashed. The Arabs forcefully entered Barcelona in 716 and it was not until 801 that the soldiers of Charlemagne's son, Louis the Pious, reconquered the city, transforming it into a Spanish March of the Frankish empire.

The massifs of Garraf thereafter became the boundaries between the Christian and Arab worlds. Wilfred the Hairy, one of the Catalan national heroes, fought the Arabs at the side of Charles the Bald. As a reward for his glorious deeds, the French king granted Barcelona its independence.

The Middle Ages under the counts of Barcelona were a period of splendor and inarrestable development for the city which traded with Genoa and Venice. After it was joined to Provence, Ramón Berenguer IV (1131-1162) married a princess of Aragon and created a solid vast kingdom in the Iberian peninsula. This was Barcelona's golden age. William the Conqueror drove the Saracens from the Balearic Islands (from Mallorca in 1235 and from Ibiza in 1238), Catalan power spread to Sicily, Corsica, Sardinia and even as far as Greece. Barcelona, the capital of Catalonia, was the leading port in the Mediterranean, the most important city in Spain, and it remained so until the discovery of America. With the opening of the new routes, its fortunes rapidly declined. The center of Spain shifted in the direction of Madrid and the southern ports. The centuries that followed were difficult. Barcelona rebelled more than once against the central government of Spain and fought against the Bourbon dynasty. It paid dearly for these acts of revolt. It lost its autonomy and the Catalan language was outlawed. Barcelona did not make a comeback until the 18th century with Charles III and then its port was reopened to trade with America and the city experienced a new and impetuous development.

During the Spanish Civil War, Barcelona was the capital of the Spanish republic for a little over a year.

3

Plaza de Cataluña.

Plaza Puerta de la Paz. ▶

# LAS RAMBLAS

«It's the most beautiful street in the world». This is how the English writer Somerset Maugham defined Barcelona's Ramblas, the most famous avenue in the Catalan capital, the most famous in all of Spain. The long shady street lined with plane trees is a promenade in the heart of the old city, a straight line, that joins two of Barcelona's vital points: Plaza de Cataluña and Plaza de la Puerta de la Paz with the column bearing the monument to Christopher Columbus. In the Ramblas traffic runs along either side of a wide stone ribbon where one can freely walk, rest, play, talk. Plaza de Cataluña is the most famous and best loved square in the city, a strategic nerve center of Barcelona. Nine of the city's principal streets encounter each other here and underground the tracks of the subway cross. Plaza de Cataluña is the downtown business and banking district of the city. It is the square which divides ancient Barcelona and the medieval quarter from the modern part of the city. Two large fountains with ornamental waterworks embellish Plaza de Cataluña, which is always crowded until late at night. Across from the avenue of the Ramblas stands a celebrated statue — *The*

*Las Ramblas: flower venders.*

*Goddess* by Joseph Clará. One of the outstanding buildings in the vicinity of the avenue of the Ramblas is the Romanesque Gothic church of **Santa Ana**, built in 1146 and restored after it was destroyed by fire in 1936. Inside is an elegant galleried *cloister* with pointed arches in its lower arcade, dating to the 14th-15th century.

The avenues of the Ramblas, over a kilometer long (1180 meters) begin at Plaza de Cataluña. The trees were planted during the Napoleonic occupation by General Duchesne who had them brought from Gerona.

Actually the Ramblas lies on the bed of a river which the Arabs called «Ram-la» and which marked the boundary of the medieval stronghold. A second circle of walls was built around old Barcelona along the course of the stream. As years went by, the buildings erected on the banks of the «Ram-la» were mostly religious in nature and what was later to become the Ramblas was at the time known as the Calle de los Conventos. It was not until 1704 that what was left of the stream began to be covered up and urbanized and that the Ramblas began to look like it does now.

«Ramblejar» is one of the favorite pasttimes of the Barcelonians. It is a neologism which means «walk along the ramblas». To walk untiringly up and down this long boulevard, back and forth between Plaza de Cataluña and the Port, stopping to discuss football or corrida is how the inhabitants of Barcelona love best to pass the time of day. The Ramblas is the beating heart, the market of the city: newsstands that look more like bookshops, cafés, venders of flowers and birds, mimes and ambulant players, sailors off duty populate this part of Barcelona at all hours of the day and night.

Actually the Ramblas is a succession of avenues, five stretches of streets with different names and aspects. The Rambla de Canaletas is the first part, right off Plaza de Cataluña. The lovely fountain almost at its beginning is magic. Legend says that whoever drinks its waters will never more leave Barcelona.

The name of the old university which Philip V transferred to Cervera still exists in the second part of the Ramblas, the Rambla de los Estudios, now occupied by the cages of the bird venders. The Baroque church of **Nuestra Señora de Belén** (Church of Bethlehem, of the

Las Ramblas: decorative pavement.

Las Ramblas: bird venders.

18th century) and the **Palacio Moya** (late 18th century) close the Rambla de los Estudios.

The liveliest and loveliest part of the Ramblas begins here: the Rambla de San José, now rebaptized Rambla de las Flores because of the dozens of flower venders to be found there. On either side is the popular **Mercado de la Boquería** (colonnades with an iron roof) and the **Palacio de la Virreina** which houses the Museo de Artes Decorativas. The Llano de la Boquería, a confusing and noisy intersection of the Ramblas, interrupts the Rambla de las Flores and is followed by the Rambla de los Capuchinos, where Barcelona's most important theater stands — the **Gran Teatro del Liceo**, next to the church of San Pablo del Campo. Calle Conde del Asalto, to the right of the Ramblas, leads to **Palacio Güell**, by Antonio Gaudí, which now houses the Museo de Arte Escénico. This small street is one of the streets bordering the Barrio Chino (the Chinese quarter).

The Rambla de Santa Mónica is the last part of the avenue and leads directly to the column of the monument to Columbus, a few steps from the entrance to the port of Barcelona.

# GRAN TEATRO DEL LICEO

One of the most famous theaters in the world, it is one of the best in Europe as far as acoustics is concerned and second only to La Scala of Milan in its seating capacity. Originally begun in 1844 on the Rambla de los Capuchinos, on the site of the Monastery of La Bona Nova which was initially built in 1638, it was based on the plans of the architect Garriga y Roca and took four years to build. After the fire of 1862, the Theater was restored by Oriol Mestres and frescoed by Alsina, Casas and Tigalt.

# PALACIO DE LA VIRREINA

Facing on the Rambla de las Flores, the palace was commissioned in 1772 from the architect Carles Grau by the Viceroy of Peru. His wife, María Francisa de Fivaller, went to live there and the palace took its name from her, vice-queen of Peru. It houses the **Museo de Artes Decorativas** and the valuable *Colecion Cambó*.

# HOSPITAL DE LA SANTA CRUZ

The Hospital de la Santa Cruz is an extraordinary ensemble of buildings in the heart of the old hospital district, not far from the Ramblas. The first four stones were laid in 1401 by religious and royal authorities on a site that had already been occupied by a hospital. The original core of the Hospital consisting of four wings around a central courtyard was finished in 1415, enlarged in 1509 and rebuilt in 1638. Eventually the hospital was transferred to more suitable quarters and the Santa Cruz ensemble was used for the Biblioteca de Cataluña.

◄ *Gran Teatro del Liceo: facade.*

*Palacio de la Virreina: exterior.*

*Hospital de la Santa Cruz: reading room in the library.*

*Plaza Real: the fountain with the Three Graces.*

*San Pablo del Campo: exterior and view of the cloister.* ▶

## PLAZA REAL

If Plaza de Cataluña is one of the nerve centers of Barcelona, Plaza Real is the romantic and popular heart of the city. Classical arches, one after the other, in the center of Barcelona's old quarters, a row of austere palaces with clear references to architecture in the French cities of the Napoleonic period, palms which rise up from the stone pavement, a fountain flanked by the Three Graces, Plaza Real is the place to seek refuge from the rush and hubbub of the Ramblas, to interrupt the interminable «ramblejar» and sit down in one of the innumerable cafés or beer halls and try the Catalan «bocadillos».

Plaza Real was planned and built by Daniel Molina who was also the author of the houses with fine porticoes which surround the Mercado de la Boquería, on the other side of the Ramblas. The great Antonio Gaudí also had a part to play in the outfitting of Plaza Real. It was one of his first works: he designed the curious lamp posts in the square. Every Sunday Plaza Real is a particularly lively spot when it becomes the philatelic and numismatic center of Barcelona.

## SAN PABLO DEL CAMPO

The exact date of the construction of the stupendous church of San Pablo del Campo is unknown. Various hypotheses have been put forward: according to some sources a community of Benedictine monks had been set up here in the fields which divided the heart of the old city from the hill of Montjuich. Their monastery was probably destroyed during the years of Arab domination.

At the beginning of the 12th century the Romanesque church of San Pablo del Campo was built on those ruins — one of the loveliest churches in Barcelona. While the main building dates back to 1117, the chapter hall and the abbot's house were built a century later. The bell tower dates to the 18th century. The architrave of the entrance *portal* is supported by columns with Visigothic capitals.

The gem of the church is its delightful *cloister*, scanned by small polylobed arches. Its loggia and garden are another refuge well known to the native Barcelonians when they want to flee from the confusion of the Barrio Chino which is adjacent to the church.

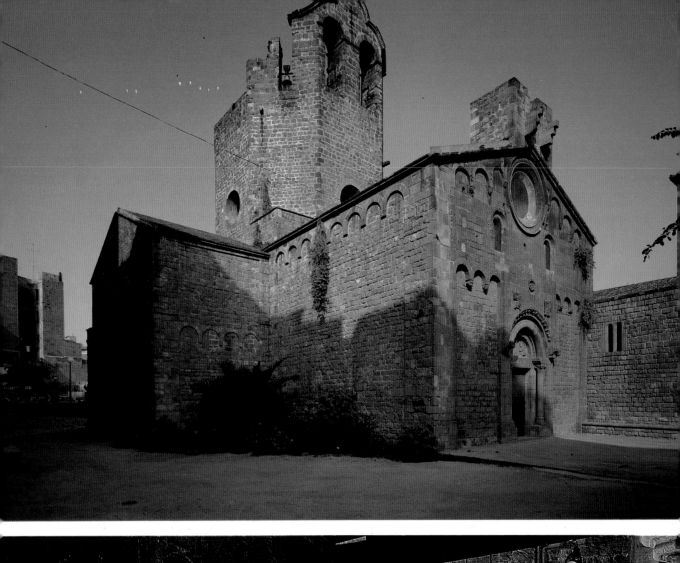

# PUERTA DE LA PAZ

The Gateway of Peace is the natural outlet for the long avenues of the Ramblas, a large square which is one of the many nerve centers of Barcelona. This square marks the boundary between the medieval city and the port and is at the crossing between Paseo de Colón and the Paralelo, on the street that rises to the castle of Montjuich.

The famous *monument to Christopher Columbus*, one of the best-known symbols of the Catalan capital, rises at the center of Plaza Puerta de la Paz. The monument commemorates the return of the Italian navigator from the shores of the New World and his meeting, after his trip, with the Spanish sovereigns in Tinell Hall in the Royal Palace of Barcelona. But fate can be ironical — the discovery of America, favored by a Catalan king, marked the beginning of the decline of the port of Barcelona.

The monument was built at the end of the 19th century after designs by Cayetano Buigas. It was inaugurated late in the spring of 1888 and consists of an iron column 59 meters high. The statue of Columbus is in bronze and not over 8 meters high. An elevator rises to the top of the column and permits a fine close-up panorama of the port of Barcelona. Some of the most important buildings in the city are situated around Plaza Puerta de la Paz: behind the monument to Columbus is the Royal Arsenal while the Customs offices are located on the opposite side of the square in a palace designed by the architect Enrique Sagnier at the end of the last century.

The Palace of the Military Governor and the Port offices are also on the Plaza Puerta de la Paz. At the entrance to the Paralelo, which joins Puerta de la Paz to Plaza de España, is part of the 15th-century walls, with the only extant gate of that stretch of the encircling walls: the Puerta de Santa Madrona.

*Plaza Puerta de la Paz: two views of the monument to Christopher Columbus.*

Maritime Museum: reconstruction of the galley of Don Juan of Austria.

# ROYAL SHIPBUILDING YARDS

The Reales Atarazanas, the huge Royal Shipyards of the great medieval Catalan navy, lie opposite the monument to Columbus, on one side of the Plaza Puerta de la Paz. The original core of the building was constructed on order of James I on the occasion of the war against the Saracens for the control of the Balearic Islands. The original building was enlarged by Peter II and completed by Peter III. This was the period in which Barcelona dominated the Mediterranean Sea, the golden period of Catalonia as a sea power. The royal shipyards worked full time for centuries: they were capable of building 30 sailing ships at a time. But with the discovery of America, the Catalan capital was excluded from the route to the New World and relegated to a subaltern role.

As time went by the naval shipyards changed owner and scope until 1941 when the city decided to install the Museo Maritimo there.

The immense rooms have permitted the reconstruction and exhibition of the flagship of the Christian fleet in the battle of Lepanto (1571) against the Turks. The royal galley of Admiral Don Juan of Austria was built

Panorama of the port.

Another view of the galley
of Don Juan of Austria.

right in the shipyards of the Catalan capital. The replica was built in 1971, the year in which Barcelona celebrated the quatercentenary of its victory.

The **Maritime Museum** collections also include archaeological finds, navigation charts, models of fishing boats and merchant ships, ceramics, original figureheads, and among other riches, an atlas of 1493 which belonged to Amerigo Vespucci.

Behind the column of the monument to Christopher Columbus a copy of the flagship of the small fleet of caravels of the great Genoese navigator is moored to the wharf of the Plaza Puerta de la Plaz. The Santa María is a faithful reproduction of 1951 and houses a floating museum.

# PASEO DE COLÓN

Paseo de Colón is Barcelona's sea-front: it skirts the entire area of the port and runs from Plaza Antonio López, at the far corner of the district of Barceloneta, to the slopes of the hill of Montjuich.

It is a large thoroughfare more than forty meters wide and despite the traffic it is possible to walk in all tranquility. It is one of Barcelona's historical sites: one of the many legends narrates that Miguel de Cervantes, the author of «Don Quixote», lived at n. 33 of Paseo de Colón and finished his masterpiece in the Catalan city. His hero too visited Barcelona and was amazed at the sombre, macabre atmosphere of those years.

From the hill of Montjuich, Paseo de Colón crosses Plaza Puerta de la Paz and reaches Plaza Duque de Medinaceli. Sober 19th-century palaces surround this tree-shaded square with its *monument to Admiral Galcerán Marquet* by Daniel Molina.

The palace of the Capitanía General, set between the old walls of the convent of the Brothers of Mercy, also lies along Paseo de Colón. The long avenue ends in Plaza Antonio Lopez, adjacent to the lovely Plaza Palacio. The *statue to López* at the center of the square is by Venancio Vallmitjana. On one side of the square is the large Post Office building.

# BASÍLICA DE LA MERCED

Very close to Paseo de Colón is a small church in Baroque style built in the second half of the 18th century, between 1765 and 1775. This is the Basilica de la Merced. Josep Mas, who designed it, utilized the old Gothic remains of the church of San Miguel and preserved a Renaissance side doorway dating to 1516. The basilica was actually the sanctuary of the Convent of the Brothers of Mercy and is now occupied by the Capitanía General.

The Basilica de la Merced is important for Barcelona because it preserves the sacred venerated image of the *Virgen de la Merced*, a small but elegant wooden statue, richly dressed in gold raiments, made in the 14th century by the wood sculptor Pere Moragues. The Virgen de la Merced, together with the «Moreneta» of Montserrat, is a protectress of Barcelona.

At the end of September, in the first days of autumn, the entire city celebrates its protectress in grandiose style. It is the finest holiday of the year, a joyous rite that is both secular and religious, which crosses over the borders of the church and explodes into the streets and squares. Plaza de San Jaime, secular heart of Barcelona, is invaded by the «Castellers», who outdo each other in daring human pyramids, and the tall manikins (the «caperudos») in papier-maché of the royal personages of Catalonia.

◄ *Paseo de Colón.*

*Basilica de la Merced: exterior.*

*Basilica de la Merced: Virgen de la Merced.*

# LONJA

Situated between Plaza de Antonio López and the lovely Plaza Palacio, at the end of the long Paseo de Colón, the Lonja houses the Stock Exchange of Barcelona and the Chamber of Commerce and Navigation.

Plaza Palacio, in the center of which is a monumental fountain decorated with allegoric statues of Italian school, is the entrance to the maritime district of the city, Barceloneta.

The facade of the Lonja, neoclassic like all the changes the building underwent, is by the architect Juan Soler Faneca, who redesigned the palace in the second half of the 18th century.

But the real history of the palace of the Lonja begins in the 14th century with the original core, built between 1380 and 1390 as a covered market, the first building of its kind in all of Spain. In the 15th century it became the headquarters for the customs offices and the naval consulate. The large *transaction hall*, the main hall of the Lonja, is all that is left of the original structure. It is a fine example of Gothic style, with three aisles and six arches which support the polychrome coffered wooden ceiling.

Noteworthy inside the palace are the garden with marble statues and the famous *staircase* of the foyer, which leads to the offices of the Chamber of Commerce and Navigation.

*Lonja: entrance staircase.*

*Lonja: Transaction Hall.*

The Cathedral of Saint Eulalia. ▶

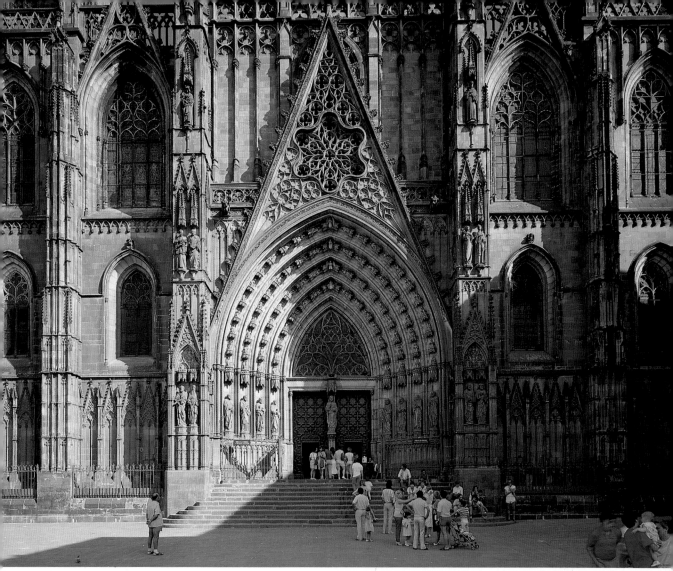

◀ *Cathedral: facade.*

*Cathedral: main portal.*

*The Sardana - a folk dance.*

# CATHEDRAL OF SAINT EULALIA

In the 4th century a small church already stood on the highest point of the old Roman colony, the small «Mons Taber». And it must have been an important church if two centuries later, as the cathedral of Barcelona, it was the setting for the Council of 559. These were times of violence and the church was destroyed by Almanzor in 985. Shortly after the year 1000 the Catalan king Ramón Berenguer I rebuilt it in Romanesque style, but plans for the great church which today rises next to the Avenida de la Catedral, in the heart of the Barrio Gótico, were only begun under James II, king of Aragon.

Construction began in 1298 and continued, until 1448, following the stylistic canons of the Catalan Gothic. An inscription near the Puerta de San Ivo, in Calle de los Condes, commemorates the date of the be-

◄ *Cathedral: interior.*

*Cathedral: the crypt.*

ginning of the work. The Cathedral was dedicated to Saint Eulalia, a legendary young girl who was tortured and killed for her Christian faith in the 4th century.

Throughout the years the building has undergone considerable modifications. The main facade of the church dates to the end of the 19th century and was quite controversial. The architects Mestres and Font were supposed to have followed the original designs of 1408 by a French architect. The central spire of the cathedral was not built until 1913.

The **interior** is grandiose and austere. The stained-glass windows date to the 15th century and illuminate the nave and two aisles which represent Catalan Gothic at its purest. The Cathedral is a real treasure chest: everything — the 26 chapels, the sacristy, the crypt with the sarcophagus of the Saint, the lovely cloister — is to be carefully visited. On one side of the main entrance is the **Capilla del Baptisterio**, with the marble baptismal fonts, by Onofre Julia, dating to 1443. On the other side is the large **Capilla de San Olegario** protected by a wrought iron railing. Above Bishop Olegarius's altar, a work by Ça-Anglada, is a wooden 16th-century *Crucifix* which Don Juan of Austria carried on the flagship of the Christian fleet in the battle of Lepanto. Beyond the Capilla de San Olegario is the **Capilla de San Clemente**, with the Gothic sepulchre of Doña Sanxa Ximénez de Cabrera and an altarpiece of the 15th century.

The presbytery, the **Capilla Mayor** of the Cathedral, opens off the transept. In the radiating chapels of the chevet there are numerous 14th and 15th century *retablos*, high expressions of Catalan art. The 15th century altarpiece of the *Visitation* is in the **Capilla de San Miguel**, and one of Bernat Martorell's masterpieces, the altarpiece of the *Transfiguration*, is in the **Capilla del Patrocinio**, while the 14th century altarpiece of the *Archangel Gabriel* is in the apse, the **Capilla del Santo Cristo**. The sixth chapel contains the altarpiece of *Saints Martin and Ambrose*, the seventh the altarpiece of the middle of the 15th century representing *Saint Claire and Saint Catherine*. The Gothic sepulchre of Bishop Ramón de Escales is to be found in the **Capilla de los Santos Inocentes**. The two sepulchres of the founders of the Cathedral, Count Ramón Berenguer I and his wife Almodis, are to be seen to the right of the high altar. To the left of the transept, the **Puerta de San Ivo**, the oldest part of the Cathedral which is still Romanesque in appearance, leads to the Calle de los Condes.

Under the Capilla Mayor, a short flight of stairs leads to the **Crypt** where the body of Saint Eulalia is preserved in an *alabaster sarcophagus* of 1327, the work of a pupil of the Italian sculptor Nicola Pisano. The German painter Müller painted the Incoronation of Saint Eulalia on the large keystone of the vault of the Crypt,

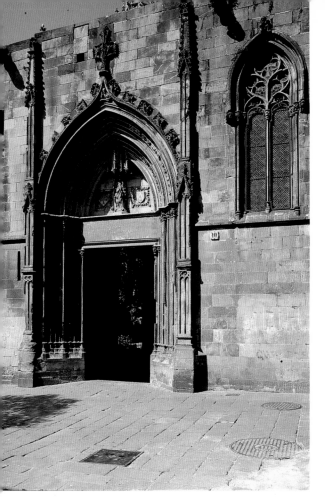

Cathedral: Puerta de Santa Eulalia.

◀ Cathedral: choir stalls.

◀ Cathedral: detail of the decoration of the stalls.

Cathedral: Puerta de la Piedad.

which was designed by Jaime Fabré.

The Renaissance enclosure of the large **Choir** is at the center of the nave. Work on the construction began in 1390 when Ramón de Escales was bishop of Barcelona, and his coat of arms (three ladders) is sculptured on the walls of the Choir. The entire enclosure is decorated with marble *bas-reliefs* which narrate the life of Saint Eulalia, begun in 1517 by Bartolome Ordoñez and Pere Vilar. Inside are the famous wooden *stalls*, decorated with gilded polychrome coats of arms of the Knights of the Order of the Golden Fleece who were convoked in the Cathedral by Emperor Charles V and Archduke Maximilian of Austria in 1519. The upper stalls and the *bishop's throne* are by Ça-Anglada, the lower row of stalls by M. Bonafé, and the crowning canopy of the stalls was created by the artists Lochner and Friedrich.

In a corner, to the right of the Capilla Mayor, is the **Sacristy** which houses the *Cathedral Treasure*. This valuable collection of liturgical objects and religious art includes a 15th-century reliquary decorated with the collar of the Order of the Golden Fleece which belonged to Charles V, the gilded chair of the Aragonese king Martin I and a gold and silver monstrance of 1390.

Access to the cloister of the cathedral is through the Puerta de San Severo, inside the church, from the Chapel of Saint Lucy, to the right of the main entrance to the cathedral, from the **Puerta de Santa Eulalia** which opens on the Calle del Obispo Irurita, and through the **Puerta de la Piedad**, in the calle of the same name, decorated in the lunette above the portal with a wooden *Pietà* in relief, of Nordic make (16th century).

The cloister, which is without doubt one of the loveliest Gothic cloisters in existence, is unique in more ways than one. One of these consists in the diversity of its components. The old chapels of the religious congregations, separated from the cloister portico by austere wrought iron railings, open off three of its four sides. The wing set against the side of the Cathedral is the oldest and dates to the 14th century, while the other wings are from the middle of the 15th century. Where the oldest wing and the one at right angles to the side of the church meet is the Romanesque **Puerta de San Severo**, in front of which is a charming old conventual washstand set at the center of a sort of temple, the **Pabellón de San Jorge**, with the vault decorated with sculpture representing St. George at the center and the Fathers of

25

◄ *Cloister: the washstand.*

*Cloister: view.*

*Cloister: loggia.*

the Church on the ribs. Every year for the feast day of «Corpus Christi», the traditional «ou com balla» (dancing egg) is held: an eggshell which «dances» suspended above the basin of the washstand on its spout of water. Near the temple is a small pond and a flock of geese, which some say are symbols of Saint Eulalia's purity. In the corner diagonally opposite the Puerta de San Severo is the Romanesque **Chapel of Saint Lucy**, or better what is left of the Romanesque cathedral (13th century). Consecrated to the Madonna in 1268, the facade boasts a fine Romanesque *portal*. Inside is the tomb of the bishop Arnau de Gurb, founder of the chapel, and that of the parish priest of Santa Coloma.

The **Chapter Hall**, adjoining the chapel, dates to the first half of the 15th century and shelters the **Cathedral Museum**, with a collection that includes the famous *Pietà* by Bartolomé Bermejo (of the 15th century), the illuminated *missal* of Saint Eulalia (by Ramón Destorrent), the *altarpiece of S. Bernardino* (15th century) by Jaime Huguet, the *Madonna and Child* (15th century) by Sano di Pietro and *Saint Onofrio* (14th century) by Jaime Serra.

*Calle del Obispo Irurita.*

*Calle del Obispo Irurita:*
*the charming suspended bridge.*

# BARRIO GÓTICO

While the Barrio Gótico, also known as «Barri de la Seu» (Cathedral quarter) or by the odd name of «rovell de l'ou» (egg yolk), may not be a district in the true sense of the word it does enclose most of what is left of medieval Barcelona and contains some of the most interesting monuments of the city. What is probably the most fascinating zone of the city includes the area between the Cathedral and the City Hall and is partially surrounded by the bastions of the Roman walls. The denomination Gothic quarter dates to the early 20th century. While other Gothic areas existed in the city, as a whole the extant buildings in this zone were more harmonious and particular care was therefore taken in their restoration. The Barrio Gótico begins in the Plaza Nueva, the oldest square in Barcelona, entrance to the solitary Roman «Barcino» and a 13th-century site of one of the most flourishing markets in the city where slaves were once sold. Two Roman towers that belonged to the old city walls which constituted the city's only defense until the 13th century are still to be found here. The **Bishop's Palace** which rises to the right of the Roman towers also dates to the 13th century and cre-

ates an interesting contrast with the modern **College of Architects**, decorated on the outside by a graffito frieze designed by Picasso. Do not be deceived by the 18th-century Baroque facade facing on Plaza Nueva for the building is actually much older and in part rests on Roman walls (incorporating one of the Roman towers as well) to which skillful restoration, particularly in the internal courtyard and the secondary facade, facing on Calle del Obispo Irurita, has restored its original dignity.

To the left of the Roman towers is another interesting building, the **Casa del Arcediano** (at present seat of the historical Archives of the City), which takes its name from the fact that it was the residence of the Archdeacon Lluis Desplá. The building, which is probably very old (11th century), was restructured throughout the centuries and is a harmonious fusion of Gothic and Renaissance styles. The interior courtyard, with a ground floor arcading of depressed arches and a moss-covered fountain at the center, is particularly lovely.

One of the three facades of the palace looks out on the famous **Calle del Obispo Irurita** (Street of the Bishop), the heart of the Barrio Gótico, which skirts the side of the Cathedral and arrives as far as Plaza de San Jaime. About halfway down, this lovely street is passed over by a charming suspended *bridge* which is a trademark for the street and connects the Palacio de la Generalidad to the secondary facade of the **Casa de los Canónigos** (House for Canons). The bridge, which is a sort of miniature summing up of Gothic art, was realized in 1926 by Juan Rubió. The Casa de los Canónigos is an enormous building with an irregular ground plan dating to the 14th century and recently restored, with a facade on Calle del Paradís. Various medieval buildings here that are open to the public house the Centro Excursionista de Cataluña and the remains of a **Roman temple** dedicated to Augustus which dates to the 2nd century. The four imposing Corinthian columns are topped by an architrave and stand on a podium. The temple was built here on the highest and most important point of the ancient «Barcino», on the very top of the «Mons Taber». On the right of Calle del Obispo Irurita, coming from Plaza Nueva, before encountering the Gothic bridge, is a narrow lane which leads to the most intimate hidden little square in the city, **Plaza de San Felipe Neri**, one of the most peaceful spots in the city (and one of the reasons why is that it is almost impossible to find and therefore rarely frequented), with a simple fountain at the center, dominated by the sober 18th-century church dedicated to San Felipe Neri. The building which shelters the Museum of the History of Shoes also faces onto the small square.

*Plaza San Felipe Neri: the church.*

Palacio de la Generalidad: main facade.

Palacio de la Generalidad: Salón de San Jorge.

Salón de San Jorge: decoration of the ceiling. ▶

# PALACIO DE LA GENERALIDAD

Plaza de San Jaime is a sort of continuation of what was once the forum of the Roman city. The ancient tradition still holds for even today the most important government buildings of Barcelona are here: the palace of the Diputación Provincial, built in various phases, beginning with the 15th century, to house the Generalidad de Cataluña (or Parliament) and the so-called Casa de la Ciudad or Ayuntamiento (the City Hall).

The main facade of the Palacio de la Generalidad, a building in Renaissance style by Pere Blay, dates to the late 16th century. The elegant secondary facade of 1416 is in Gothic style. It faces on the lovely Calle del Obispo Irurita and is the work of the architect Marc Safont. But the finest part of the building is the ancient internal *courtyard*, access to which is through a wide depressed arch. It was also built in the Catalan Gothic style by Safont (1425) and is a perfect example of the aristocratic patio of the period. A staircase, supported by a single

Palacio de la Generalidad:
Patio de los Naranjos.

Palacio de la Generalidad:
courtyard.

arch and with a finely decorated balustrade, leads to the main floor of the building where a loggia of ogee arches on slender columns looks out on the courtyard. A bold architectural solution has been found for the corner at the top of the staircase: two round-headed arches (instead of pointed arches) are set side by side, separated only by a capital without a column which, like a stalactite, is suspended in the void. Once past this fascinating «entrance» we come face to face with the admirable **Chapel of St. George**, also by Safont (1432).

The loggia of the main floor leads to the *Salón de San Jorge*, realized at the end of the 16th century by Pere Blay, which occupies the central part of the palace. It is a vast room with three aisles and vaults, supported by square pilasters, and with a dome at the center decorated with frescoes of historical subjects executed in the 1920s by Josep Mongrell.

The courtyard loggia also leads to the famous *Patio de los Naranjos* (Orange Tree Courtyard) executed between 1526 and 1600 and a good example of the transition from Gothic to Renaissance architecture. It in turn leads to the Salón del Consistorio Mayor or Salón Dorado (Gilded Hall), so-called because of the gilded ceiling. The wooden coffers of the ceiling also contain the carved and painted portraits of the Catalan kings.

Palacio de l'Ayuntamiento: the secondary facade.

Palacio de l'Ayuntamiento:
the Salón del Consejo de Ciento.

# AYUNTAMIENTO

The neoclassic facade of the palace is the result of a 19th-century restructuration of the original Gothic building. On one side, in the Calle de la Ciudad, the old Gothic *facade*, realized at the end of the 14th century by Arnau Bargués, can still be seen. The entrance portal is marked by a fine arch in relief which, on the right, «trespasses» into a wing of the palace that is at right angles to the facade, creating an original aesthetic solution. Above the arch are the coats of arms of Barcelona and Catalonia and the statue of the *archangel Raphael*.

The *Salón del Consejo de Ciento* is on the main floor of the building. It was created by Pere Llobet for the City Council of the Hundred in the 14th century and was inaugurated in the session of August 17, 1373 and enlarged in the middle of the 19th century. From here access to the 19th-century *Salón de la Reina Regente* — so-called because of the portrait of the queen Maria Cristina with her son, the small Alfonso XIII, which hangs there — where the City Council normally meets. The main floor also contains the evocative *Salón de las Crónicas*, of the first half of the century, almost completely frescoed by José Sert with historical scenes.

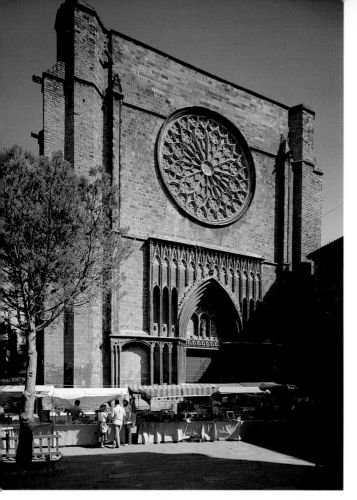

Santa María del Pino: facade.

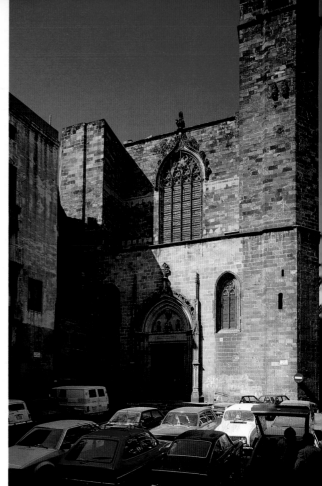

Santos Justo y Pastor: facade.

# SANTA MARÍA DEL PINO

Known also as Nuestra Señora de los Reyes and rising on the site of a religious building of the 10th century, the construction of the church began in 1322 (utilizing in part precedent structures, such as the 13th-century side portal) and it was consecrated in 1453, although the crypt is 16th century. A large rose window stands out against the simple rigor of the Gothic facade. Of fine polychrome stained glass, it is of modern make and is what characterizes the building. Inside, a single wide nave flanked by chapels preserves a tomb dated 1394.

The church stands on one side of the square of the same name, a small intimate corner which every so often is given over to an amusing little market. The entire area around the church — the well known quarter of the Pine — is full of cafés, places in which to pass the time of day and pastry shops, which occupy rooms that are often very old, antique shops or boutiques which deal in specialized products such as masks, maps, etc. A walk along Calle de Petritxol, which leads to the church square, gives you an idea of the charm of a typical Barcelona calle and in addition provides an opportunity for tasting the best known local titbits.

# SANTOS JUSTO Y PASTOR

Another interesting building in the Barrio Gótico, this very old church is mentioned in sources as far back as the year 801 and is situated on Plaza Santo Justo together with various other Gothic buildings. The church as it is now dates back to the 14th-15th century. The simple facade is flanked by only one of the two bell towers originally planned. **Inside**, a single nave has side chapels decorated with reliefs. The *retablo* of San Felix is in the Capilla de San Felix. An estimable work by the Portuguese Pedro Núñez, it dates to the first half of the 16th century. The two holy water stoups were originally Gothic capitals.

According to the directives of the city statutes of 1282, the church of Santos Justo y Pastor has the power of conceding the privilege «de los Testamentos Sacramentales» (The Right of Sacramental Wills), which is still valid and according to which the last will of a dying person, verbally pronounced, becomes legally valid, even in the absence of written documents, if it is repeated, under oath and within six months, before the altar in the chapel of San Felix, by the witnesses present when it was formulated.

*Palacio del Lugarteniente:*
*the staircase in the courtyard.*

*A stretch of the Roman walls.*

# PALACIO DEL LUGARTENIENTE

The majestic Plaza del Rey, once the central part of the Palacio Real Mayor, residence first of the counts of Barcelona and then of the kings of Aragon, is at the very center of the city's Gothic district. Facing on the square are the Palacio del Lugarteniente («Palau del Lloctinent»), the tower known as **Mirador del Rey Martin** (a suggestive building of the middle of the 16th century with five superimposed galleries), the **Salón del Tinell**, the great hall of the palace of the counts, 14th century), the **chapel of Santa Águeda** (the 14th century Palatine chapel) and the 16th century **Casa Padellás** in which the *Historical Museum of the City* is installed. The Palace of the Lieutenant or Viceroy, whose secondary facade overlooks the square, is a sober 16th century building erected by Antonio Carbonell in 1549. It contains the Archives of the Crown of Aragon, over 4 million documents, dating back as far as the 9th century.

Worthy of note is the characteristic patio with several orders of superposed loggias and the airy main staircase, with its splendid coffered ceiling.

# THE ROMAN WALLS

The Barrio Gótico, contrary to expectations, does not consist only of buildings that date to the 13th and 14th centuries, for considerable Roman remains that date back to the 4th century A.D. are to be found in their midst.

The remains in question are what is left of the city walls built by the Romans after having reconquered the old «Barcino» which had been occupied and destroyed by the Barbarians in the second half of the 3rd century A.D. These walls, which were 1270 meters long, were about 9 meters high, about 3.50 meters thick and had strong polygonal towers and entrance gates set at intervals. The remains of a basilical building of the same period as the walls have been brought to light under the Cathedral and part of the initial structure of a Roman acqueduct as well as a stretch of walls were found in the Cathedral square. Remains of the encircling walls can still be seen in Calle Correio Viejo, Bajada Cassador, Calle Subteniente Navarro, Plaza del Ángel, Bajada Llibrería, Calle Tapinería, Plaza Berenguer III and Calle de los Condes de Barcelona, which skirts the side of the Cathedral.

Plaza Ramón Berenguer

**Plaza Ramón Berenguer el Grande**, which is at the eastern edge of the enclosing walls that are incorporated into the royal palace, creates a sort of narrow garden at the foot of the walls. Here, in Vía Layetana, stands the *equestrian monument to the count-king Ramón Berenguer III* (1082-1131), a member of the family of the Ramón who reconstructed the Cathedral of the city in 1058. The monument is set against the backdrop of the Roman walls and the side of the chapel of **Santa Águeda**.

This palatine chapel of the Palacio Real Mayor stands on the site of an old oratory of Santa María and was built on the old Roman walls. The single tall nave, scanned by ogee arches at intervals, has a fine polychrome wooden coffered ceiling. The coats of arms of James II and his wife Blanche of Anjou can still be seen in the apse and one of the masterpieces of old Catalan painting is set above the high altar, the retablo representing the Adoration of the Magi (at the center, below) and the Crucifixion (at the center, above), surrounded by six stories. The altarpiece was painted by Jaime Huguet in 1464 and is known as «*Retablo del Condestable*» because it was commissioned by the Constable Don Pedro of Portugal, one of the pretenders to the crown of Catalonia-Aragon. Vía Layetana is one of the most important urban arteries of the city and crossing the oldest quarter of Barcelona it joins the «old city» to the harbor. Evenings the panorama from here is spectacular: the majestic complex of the walls and of the chapel of Santa Águeda, with the Mirador and the bell tower of the Cathedral rising up over them, are brightly illuminated and form a fantastic backdrop.

◀ *Museo Marés: two rooms.*

*Palacio Llió: the patio.*

# MUSEO MARÉS

This museum is in an annex of the Palacio Real Mayor. The initial core of the collections was created by the sculptor Frederic Marés Deulovol, who donated it to the city of Barcelona in 1940. The exhibitions deal particularly with medieval sculpture, not only Catalan, but also from other regions of Spain. The collections on the ground floor of the museum range from a panorama of ancient Iberian, Greek and Punic sculpture to 15th-century Castilian statuary and Aragonese sculpture. Of particular interest is a rich *collection of crucifixes* of the 14th-15th centuries and one of enameled or painted *crosses* in wood or metal from the Gothic period to the 17th century. The sculpture and painting exhibited on the first floor range from the early Middle Ages to the 19th century. The Madonna and Child was a common theme in 15th century sculpture while the Holy Family appears often in 13th to 16th century work. The examples of Spanish Renaissance sculpture clearly document the Italian and Flemish influences. Particularly interesting from this point of view is a group of sculptures in alabaster (reliefs representing the *Annunciation*, the *Visitation*, the *Adoration of the Shepherds* and the *Presentation in the Temple*, by Francisco Giralte) and a *Virgin and Child* attributed to Alonso Berruguete.

# CALLE DE MONTCADA

Calle Princesa, a street off the large Vía Layetana, leads to Calle de Montcada, originally little more than a path along the banks of a brook, but honored with the name of «Vía Nova» when the first buildings began to rise just outside the old city walls. The present name derives from Guillermo Ramón de Montcada who built his palace there in 1153.

From the 13th to the 18th century this street was at the height of its splendor and was one of the most aristocratic in the city thanks to the rich mansions which were built on either side. This all ended in the 19th-century when the high society of the time preferred other areas of Barcelona.

One of the old houses that still stands in this street at n. 12, is the **Palace of the Marqués de Llió**, a fine 16th-century building, now owned by the city which has installed the *Museo de Indumentaría* (Costume Museum) there, realized thanks to the generous bequest of Manuel Rocamora. The three floors of the palace contain exhibitions of liturgical vestment, dolls, shoes, costume accessories (fans and purses), matador costumes, tapestries, uniforms, examples of fine embroidery. The oldest objects date to the 16th century, the most recent are 20th-century.

*Museo Picasso: «El niño enfermo».*

*Museo Picasso: «Harlequin».* ▶

# MUSEO PICASSO

**Palacio Berenguer de Aguilar,** a 14th-century building with a fine Gothic patio, is at n. 15 Calle de Montcada. It was the residence of the Llinás family and then of the counts of Santa Coloma who modified the original Gothic structure of the building in Renaissance and Baroque style. It is now the home of the *Picasso Museum,* and the three floors are given over to the donation of Jaime Sabartés, a friend of the painter's, and the donation Picasso himself made, consisting of several hundred oil paintings, sketches, drawings and etchings. The space was insufficient for all these works and the collection overflowed into the Castellet palace, a 17th-century building adjoining the Berenguer de Aguilar palace. The quantity and variety of the material on exhibit (arranged chronologically) make this museum a unique and indispensable instrument in understanding

*Casa Dalmases: the patio.*

*Santa María del Mar: panorama at night.* ▶

the work of the great artist — from one of his first attempts (a drawing done when he was nine years old) to the works painted towards the end of the century, in La Coruña, the production of his two sojourns in Barcelona (from 1895 to 1897 and from 1901 to 1904), the famous «blue period» (after his stay in Paris), his cubist experiments, up to the paintings done in Cannes in 1957. To mention only a few of the masterworks here, there is the large oil painting, *Science and Charity,* done by the master when he was barely fifteen, *El Paseo Colón* and *Barcelona* (dedicated to the city he loved so much), *El niño enfermo* (blue period) and Harlequin (1917, cubist period). A whole section of the museum is dedicated to the 58 paintings which Picasso donated to the museum in 1968, 44 of which are variations on the theme of *Las Meninas,* the famous painting by Velázquez in the Prado.

## CASA DALMASES

Continuing along Calle de Montcada, the Dalmases house at n. 20 is one of those aristocratic residences which help to make this street so charming. Even if it is not perfectly preserved, the 17th-century palace with its fine Baroque patio and family chapel with a vault decorated in relief on the piano nobile stands out among the others in all its splendor. Built as the residence of Pablo Ignacio de Dalmases, it was later also the seat of the «Academia dels Desconfiats» (Academy of the Diffident).

## SANTA MARÍA DEL MAR

The apse of the church of Santa María del Mar lies at the end of Calle de Montcada. The street and the church have been declared national monuments, for it is one of the most important examples of medieval Catalan architecture. In the first half of the 14th century, after having occupied Sardinia, Alfonso IV had the building of the church begun, in fulfillment of a vow previously made by James I, the Conqueror. The architect Berenguer de Montagut built it on the site of a precedent parish church of the 10th century, and it was terminated under Peter III, in 1383. The exterior of the church is majestic with its wide flat surfaces, fine splayed portal, harmonious tall pointed-arch windows and two slender octagonal bell towers crowned by three

Santa María del Mar: main portal.

Santa María del Mar: interior. ▶

orders of windows. The lovely flamboyant Gothic *rose window* which decorates the upper part of the facade is the result of a revision carried out in the second half of the 15th century after the original window had been destroyed in 1428.

Stylistically the nave and two narrow aisles of the **interior** are unusually unified and are supported by octagonal piers. There are so few of these that they are 13 meters apart, a surprisingly great interval for Gothic cathedrals and one of the particular characteristics of

the building. Some of the elegant *stained-glass windows*, of the 15th century, are also noteworthy (the Last Judgement in the left aisle, the Ascension of the Virgin in one of the side chapels, and above all the Coronation of the Virgin at the center of the rose window on the facade).

Unfortunately the fire of 1936 almost completely destroyed the decoration of the interior and the high altar, an estimable Baroque work of the second half of the 18th century.

# LA CIUDADELA

The large park of the city of Barcelona, the Ciudadela, lies at the end of the Avenida del Marqués de Argentera, between the district of Barceloneta and the Paseo de San Juan. The Ciudadela is a splendid green area covering more than 700 acres: tree-shaded avenues, palms, fields, terraces, statues, flower gardens, pools and lakes, waterfalls and palaces form a mosaic created according to the classical criteria of landscape architecture of the late 19th century.

It was called Ciudadela because Philip V had a military fortress built here between 1715 and 1718. The Bourbon king, who had won the War of Succession to the throne of Spain, decided to punish Barcelona for having sided with his adversaries. After the conquest of the city, which took place in 1714, the new sovereign dissolved the Catalan parliament, officially prohibited the Catalan language and razed one of the residential districts, the Ribera, to the ground. More than 10,000 inhabitants had lived here and this was where he built the fortified bastions of the Ciudadela.

The Ciudadela existed not much more than a century. In 1808 the French took over the fortification, and it was not until 1869 that the land on which nothing but ruins remained was restored to the city of Barcelona. The idea for a city park took form in those years. The project was by the architect José Fontseré with the collaboration of José Vilaseca, but it was not until 1888, when the World Fair was held in the gardens of the Ciudadela, that the park acquired its present luxurious aspect.

The **Arch of Triumph** was built then as the entrance to the Exposition. It stands at the end of the Paseo de San Juan and is a showy structure of Mudéjar inspiration (the Arab-Christian art which developed after the 12th century), designed and built by José Vilaseca. At the top of the arch (30 meters high) is an impressive frieze by Josep Llimona.

The arch leads to Paseo Salón de Victor Pedrera. On the left rises the **Palacio de Justicia**, a piece of modern architecture (1911) by Sagnier and Domenech Estepá. Inside, in the hall of the «Pasos Perdidos», murals by José Sert can be seen.

The large tree-shaded avenue leads to the heart of the park of the Ciudadela. One of the main buildings was originally the old city Arsenal, which, as time went by, was transformed into the Royal Palace and the seat of the **Catalan Parliament**. Today this neoclassic building houses the **Museo de Arte Moderno**.

The museum collections are concerned with Catalan sculpture and painting of the 19th and 20th centuries. Many pictures by the Tarragonian painter Mariano Fortuny are exhibited here side by side with Isidro Nonell's delicately colored works and paintings by José Sert. Joan Miró, Salvador Dalí (a portrait of his father) and the surrealism of Antonio Tapies are also represented in the Museo de Arte Moderno. The famous *Numismatic Cabinet* and the curious *Gallery of Illustrious Catalans* are installed in one wing of the museum. In front of the building the statue of a white nude by Josep Llimona, «Desolation» («*Desconsol*»), stands in the midst of a small pool with waterlilies.

One of the most spectacular attractions of the Ciudadela is the fountain known as *Cascada Monumental*, a grandiose redundant example of Catalan neoclassic taste. It was designed and executed by the architect of the Ciudadela, José Fontseré, but a young university student, at his beginnings and still unaware of his great future, by the name of Antonio Gaudí, also contributed to the work. The fountain of the Cascada Monumental is decorated with statues by Venancio

*Ciudadela: Museo de Arte Moderno.*

*Ciudadela: Arch of Triumph.*

*Ciudadela: the Cascada Monumental.*

*Ciudadela: another view of the park.*

*Ciudadela: the fountain with
the Lady with the Parasol.*

Vallmitjana, while the ensemble of Aurora's quadriga
on top is by Rosendo Nobás.

Numerous other buildings rise around the central
core of the Ciudadela. A sort of medieval **castle** (actually
an austere palace in red brick decorated with
crenellation and coats of arms in stone) houses the collections of the **Zoological Museum**. The building, situated at the end of Viale dei Tigli, was designed by the
architect Domenech y Montaner. The museum is dedicated above all to the naturalistic patrimony of
Catalonia.

. Not far from the Zoological Museum, between the
greenhouses of the Umbráculo and the Invernáculo, is
the Geological Museum, the fine **Museo Martorell** with
its valuable collections of minerals and palaeontology.

Barcelona's **Zoological Garden**, with a never-ending

*Palacio de la Musica Catalana: foyer and staircase.*

flow of visitors, is also to be found in the park of the Ciudadela. A small statue at the entrance to the zoo, representing Saint Francis of Assisi, is by Pedro Jou.

Statues are to be found throughout the park. In the long walks through the Ciudadela one is likely to come face to face with the *statue of Rius y Taulet* (at the entrance to the Paseo Lluis Companys), mayor of Barcelona in the period of the 1888 World Fair and its sagacious promotor, as well as a *bronze group of gazelles* by Nuria Tortras, dedicated to Walt Disney. Another famous statue in the Ciudadela is the **equestrian monument to General Prim**, a copy by Puigjaner of the original by Frederic Marés which stood in the exact same place. Note should also be taken of the statue that commemorates the *Catalan Volunteers* of World War I.

But the most famous statue in the Ciudadela is an elegant and charming lady shading herself from the sun with a parasol. The *Dama del Paraguas* is in the Zoological Garden, surely one of the most romantic of the many symbols of Barcelona and deserving of the thousand ornamental waterworks and tree-lined avenues in the Ciudadela. The lady was sculptured by Roig y Soler in 1888 and is set above a simple fountain with two basins.

# PALACIO DE LA MUSICA CATALANA

For a long time this building was a bone of contention but today it is justly held to be one of the outstanding examples of the art that developed in Barcelona at the end of the 19th century.

A group of enthusiastic young artists, including Vilaseca, Berenguer, Cadafalck, Martorell and, especially, Lluis Domenech y Montaner, the architect who designed this building, animated by an ardent desire to promote an aesthetic and stylistic renewal in the ambit of the Catalan «renaixença», organized numerous artistic manifestations which led to varied brilliant exhibitions. Built in 1908, today this palace is the largest concert hall in Barcelona, seat of the famous «Orfeó Català», a magnificent setting for the most important musical manifestations of the city.

The decoration is purest Art Nouveau with a generous use of colored glass, polychrome glazed tiles, mosaics, sinuous wrought iron. Altogether the effect is fantastic and theatrical and the atmosphere is one of enchantment.

49

◄ *Two views of the port.*

*Plaza de España.*

# THE PORT

The second largest city in Spain for population, Barcelona is the country's leading center of business and industry. The port is the heart of the business city: the 700 acres of the harbor area which make Barcelona an important Mediterranean seaport stretch out between the district of Barceloneta and the hill of Montjuich. Every year 17 million tons of goods, above all wine, oil, wool and sugar for exportation and corn, cotton and coal as imports, pass through the port.

The economical importance of Barcelona as a seaport was hard won. For centuries the capital of Catalonia was the principal Mediterranean port but the discovery of America changed things. The city was excluded from the new route to the New World and went into a grave decline. It was not until the second half of the 18th century when Charles III allowed her to trade with the Americas that Barcelona made a comeback.

Small boats called «golondrinas» (swallows) are used for pleasant outings in the port area. They are anchored at the wharves in Plaza Puerta de la Paz, behind the monument to Columbus.

# PLAZA DE ESPAÑA

One of the most convulsive and noisy intersections in all of Barcelona, Plaza de España is situated at the crossing of Gran Vía and the «Paralelo» (Calle del Marqués del Duero). An immense, impressive square, overflowing with traffic, Plaza de España was the monumental entrance to the old fair quarters in the World Fair of 1929.

The Catalan architect Jujol, one of Gaudí's best pupils, placed a monumental *fountain* at the center of the square. The three statues by Oslé which decorate it on three sides symbolically represent the waters of the three seas which bathe the coasts of Spain — the Mediterranean, the Bay of Biscay (or Mare Cantabricum) and the Atlantic Ocean.

The principal airlines have their headquarters in Plaza de España and the second Plaza de Toros in Barcelona, *Las Arenas*, is situated at the departure point of the Iberia terminal. Las Arenas was built at the beginning of the century and seats up to 15,000 spectators. The three massive red brick buildings in the plaza were the hotels which housed the visitors to the 1929 Exposition.

Palacio Nacional: main facade.

The Magic Fountain... ▶
«a never-ending rainbow».

# PALACIO NACIONAL

Two unusual bell towers in pure Venetian style comprise the entrance to the old enclosure of the fair quarters of the 1929 World Exposition. The two towers lead to the wide Avenida de la Reina Maria Cristina, an enormous avenue designed by the architect Raventós. The perspective of the boulevard is daring: the various buildings of the fair lead rapidly one after the other from Plaza de España up to the extraordinary ornamental waterworks of the fountain by Carlos Buigas. In the background on the slopes of the hill of Montjuich, rises the austere mass of the Palacio Nacional, which is faced in the distance by the mount on which the sanctuary of Tibidabo rises.

The fountain, situated at the foot of the flight of stairs that leads to the Palacio National, is by an engineer, Carlos Buigas. Known simply as «Luminous Fountain», it is also called *Magic Fountain* of Barcelona. And rightly so: on hot summer nights its ornamental waterworks and lights illuminate the entire city with the kaleidoscope of its reflections. The number of variations and

imaginative combinations possible come close to thirty: a chromatic mosaic, an unending rainbow.

The Magic Fountain is also the fountain of fantastic numbers: two concentric basins at different heights make up the main body; the water arrives at the fountain at the rate of 2430 liters a second; the jet of water touches on and at times exceeds fifty meters in height. Pumps and fans using 1413 horsepower and 4730 lamps employing 1445 kilowatts are an indication of the energy needed to set it in motion. In this personal version of «Sons et Lumière» Barcelona has outdone itself. From a cabin, a man using remote control directs the play of lights in the Magic Fountain all summer long.

At the top of the steps leading up from the enchantment of the fountain lies the Palacio Nacional, whose rooms contain the collections of the *Museo de Arte de Cataluña*. The Palacio Nacional was also designed by the engineer Buigas for the International Exposition of 1929. When the fair was held it housed the section dedicated to electricity.

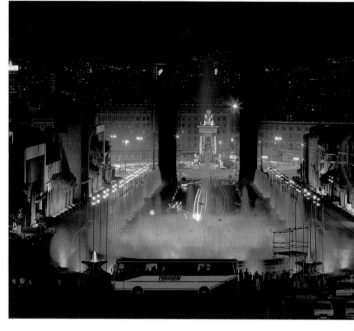

*Museo de Arte de Cataluña: exterior.*

*Museo de Arte de Cataluña:* ▶
*Christ Pantokrater (12th cent.).*

# MUSEO DE ARTE DE CATALUÑA

Situated on the hill of Montjuich, in a position which dominates the underlying Plaza de España, the Palace of the World Exposition (1929) can be reached via a monumental staircase which departs from the main avenue of the park.

The Museo de Arte de Cataluña, housed on the ground floor of this palace, is probably the richest in the world as far as Romanesque Catalan art is concerned and is without doubt one of the most important for its collections of Gothic panel paintings and sculpture. Created by Luis Pellicer, it was enlarged by his

successor Joaquín Folch y Torres, who also enriched it with numerous frescoes from various religious buildings in northern Catalonia. The works of art are exhibited in chronological order and some of the rooms in the museum, with the aid of photographic documentation, illustrate the technique used to remove the frescoes from their original sites. The more important works preserved in the rooms dedicated to Romanesque art include the frescoes from the church of San Juan de Bohí (*Martyrdom of St. Stephen*), the detached frescoes from the apse of the church of San Clemente in Tahull, repre-

senting *Christ Pantokrator,* the *Virgin and the Apostles* (12th cent.), and those from the churches of Santa María de Tahull, Santa María de Aneu and San Ginestarre de Cardós (12th cent.). A group of works attributed to the so-called Maestro de Pedret, datable to the 11th-12th century and characterized by motifs close to Byzantine art, are also of particular interest.

Noteworthy among the many wooden altar frontals in the museum are the one from Santa María de Tahull in polychrome relief (12th cent.) representing God the Father in Majesty, the one from Valltarga, and the one from Soriguerola, which already marks the passage from the Romanesque to the Gothic. This later period is well represented by a fine series of retablos, including the one from Santa Coloma de Queralt attributed to

Juan de Tarragona, and the *retablo de Sigera,* by the Serra brothers.

The most significant moments in Catalan art are represented by Luis Borrassá (*Resurrection,* first half of the 15th cent.), with whom Catalan art became receptive to various international influences; Luis Dalmau, who was influenced by Flemish art (*Altarpiece of the Councilors,* 1445), and the famous Jaime Huguet (1436-1486), skilful interpreter of Flemish naturalism in the ambit of Catalan art at the end of the 15th century (*Consecration of St. Augustine*).

Spanish painting of the 16th and 17th centuries is also well represented, with works by Pedro Berruguete, Velázquez, El Greco, Ribera (*Martyrdom of St. Bartholomew*) and Zurbarán.

# PUEBLO ESPAÑOL

The Pueblo Español is a sort of amusing Spain-in-miniature spread out over two hectares on the hill of Montjuich. The entire village can be visited. The streets, plazas, houses and buildings faithfully reproduce various important characteristic Gothic and Renaissance corners of cities or places in Catalonia, Aragon, Andalusia, Galicia, Castile, the Balearic Islands, Navarre and Estremadura. It was created for the 1929 World Fair by Xavier Nogués, Miguel Utrillo and Ramón Raventós. The replicas, realized and arranged with a truly surprising attention to detail, provide a complete anthology of Spanish architecture and of the extremely diverse architectural features of the regions of the north, the south, the mountains and the coast. Two

*Pueblo Español, in this page:*
*Puerta de San Vicente and Plaza Mayor; in the following page, from top to below and from left to right: the bell tower of the church of Utebo, a view of the Andalusian quarter, a balcony in Calle del Alcade de Zalamea and another view of the Andalusian quarter.*

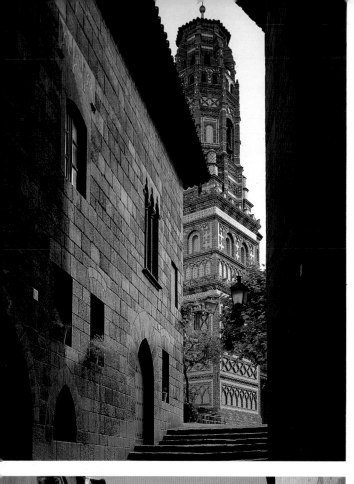

*Pueblo Español: the steps of Santiago.*

impressive towers of the *Puerta de San Vicente* mark the entrance to the village. The circle of walls which encloses the village and which reproduces the walls of the city of Avila begins here. On the other side of the gate is «Plaza Castellana», to the right of which, in «Calle de la Conquista», stand the buildings inspired by the constructions of Cáceres. Passing under the portico of Sangüesa, we come to the *Plaza Mayor*, surrounded by buildings that are typical of Guadalajara, Madrid, Segovia, Santander, etc. The square also contains the reproduction of the city hall of Valderrobles. To the left of the Plaza Mayor, after «Calle del Acalde de Zalamea» are the so-called *steps of Santiago* and other massive looking Galician buildings while further on, in «Plaza Aragonesa», the bell tower of the church of Utebo in a picturesque Mudéjar style rises to the sky. The charming reconstruction of the candid Andalusian quarter begins here, followed by that of the Catalan quarter where an old pharmacy is also reproduced. On the other hand, retracing one's steps to Plaza Mayor and turning into «Calle de los Caballeros», the road leads to the quarter dedicated to the simple and austere rural buildings of Castile, beyond which are those that recall the Basque dwellings and those of Navarre.

Plaza Mayor is often an outstanding setting for exhibitions and folklore festivals. Casa Pallaresa on the plaza shelters one of the most important museums in the village, the Spanish section of the Ethnological Museum, the *Museum of Folk Art and Industry*, dedicated to the habits, customs and traditions of Catalonia.

The village abounds in small shops specialized in the sale of typical regional products where, under the eyes of the visitor, craft objects in clay, glass, wrought iron and wood are made.

A visit to the Romanesque *Monastery* beyond the city walls is well worthwhile. Its frescoes repeat the typical pictorial decoration of the small Catalan churches in the Pyrenees.

*Some views of the most recent sports grounds of the city.*

# BARCELONA OLYMPIC CITY

Thanks to the proclamation of Barcelona as the site of the 1992 Olympic Games, the metropolis has witnessed the achievement of great reforms and improvements.

One of the most surprising results is undoubtedly the construction of the district known as Nova Icària. This new district is part of one of the four Olympic areas, that of the Parc de Mar. For the entire duration of the Games it will house the Olympic Village, where the participating athletes and their managers will be put up. The complex will be equipped with lodgings, basic services such as messes, the hospital, shops, meeting rooms, a press center, a sports pavilion.

The Nautical Base of Nova Icària will be the setting for the sailing competitions. The table tennis competitions will be held near the North Terminal (Estació del Nord). At the Frontó Colom on the other hand one of the three demonstration sports, handball, can be followed.

The nerve centre of the Olympic Games of Barcelona '92 will be, without the shadow of a doubt, the area of Montjuich, a hill intimately connected to the lives of the Barcelonians. It has been thoroughly reurbanized so as to host most of the sport facilities needed for the Olympic Games. Olympic Ring is the name given to the reurbanization project of an extensive area of the cliff, integrated into the city.

Thanks to the appointment of '92, the old stadium, originally built for the 1929 Universal Exposition, has been restructured while maintaining the original facade.

Now Olympic, the Estadí will be the stage for the inauguration and closing ceremonies of the '92 Olympics, and the athletic contest and the finals for the individual jump trials will also take place here. The Sant Jordi Palace (Palau Sant Jordi), by the architect Arata Isozaki, was basically created for sport gymnastics and rhythmic dancing, and for the handball and volley ball finals of the Games, can also host an enormous variety of sport and exibitions activities. Two new swimming pools have been built, one for the diving competitions and other for water polo, located where the municipal swimming pool was to be found and the Bernat Picornell, where the finals of water polo, swimming and synchronized swimming will be held. The Pavilion of Industrial Spain (Pavelló de la Espanya Industrial) will be the theatre for the competitions of weightlifting. Flencing will be held in the Palace of Metallurgy (Palau de la Metallurgica). The Pavilion of the Institute of Physical Education of Catalonia (Pavelló de l'Institut Nacional d'Educació Fisica de Catalunya) is also of recent date, and the Greco-Roman and free style wrestling competitions will be held there. The Area of Montjuich is supplemented by the structures of the fair complex and the Municipal Palace of Sport (Palau Municipal d'Esports), where some of the volley ball games will be disputed.

The installations which form part of Area de la Diagonal are to be found in the upper part of the city. The New Field (Camp Nou) and the Sarrià Stadium (Es-

tadí de Sarrià) will host some of the football games. The obstacle races will be held in the Ministadium (Miniestadí) of the FC Barcelona. The RC de Polo will house the services connected with the Equestrian Center. The female handball tournaments will take place in the Municipal Pavilion (Pavelló Municipal) of the CE Hospitalet del Nord. Blaugrana Palace (Palau Blaugrana) will act as setting for judo, thus completing, together with numerous hotels and meeting halls on the University campus of Barcelona, the facilities of the Area de la Diagonal.

The fourth area chosen in the popular quarter of Vall d'Hebron is centred around the Municipal Velodrome (Velòdrom Municipal), where bycicle races and volley ball contests will be disputed. In the Archery Field (Camp de Tir amb Arc) Vall d'Hebron archery contests will be held while tennis matches will take place at the Club Municipal Teixonera.

# MUSEO ARQUEOLÓGICO

The collections of the Archaeological Museum are exhibited in the 1929 World Fair Palace of Graphic Arts situated in the park of Montjuich.

The Museum is dedicated to the ancient civilizations of the Mediterranean, and its collections fill more than 30 rooms where the finds are chronologically arranged, ranging in time from prehistory to the 8th century. In the first rooms the prehistoric period is represented by finds from Catalonia, other parts of Spain, France and the Balearic Islands. Particularly interesting are the objects from Ampurias, the Greco-Roman city on the Costa Brava inhabited by the Phoenicians (6th cent. B.C.), the Hellenistic statue of Aesculapius (4th cent. B.C.), the *head of Venus* (another example of 4th-century Hellenistic art), the splendid *Roman mosaic of Iphigenia* and numerous finds from Roman Barcelona (the mosaic pavements of the ancient baths and a colonnade that has been completely reconstructed). Outstanding in the last rooms is, among others, the reconstruction of the Constantinean Mausoleum of Centcelles, the finds from the ancient «Baetulo» (Badalona), some Early Christian sarcophagi and precious examples of Visigothic gold jewellery.

# MUSEO ETNOLÓGICO Y COLONIAL

The collections of the Ethnological Museum are housed in a modern building set in the midst of the gardens of the park of Montjuich. The museum exhibits artifacts, objects of daily use, products of the crafts, and costumes from Oceania, various regions of Asia, Africa and the Americas, collected throughout the centuries in the course of the numerous Spanish expeditions.

*Museo Archeológico: statue of Aesculapius.*

*Museo Archeológico: main entrance.* ▶

*Ethnological Museum: exterior.* ▶

The modern complex of the Fundación Miró.

Fundación Miró: two rooms of the museum.

# FUNDACIÓN JOAN MIRÓ

Someone said: «Joan Miró is the night, silence, music». This definition appealed to one of the greatest artists of our century for in it Joan Miró recognized himself. He was born in Barcelona on the 20th of April 1893 in Passatge del Crédit, number 4. The capital of Catalonia and all of the Catalonian land left its mark. Chagall, the Russian painter in exile in Paris, one day wrote him: «You are lucky, my boy, you have a country». But Joan Miró never tolerated the fact that art books or encyclopedias defined him as a «Spanish painter». He sent unending letters of protest, demanded and succeeded in being defined as a «Catalan painter».

Joan Miró began to paint at an early age. A friend of Picabia, Max Ernst and André Masson, impassioned habitué of the Dadaists, he knew Hemingway, Ezra Pound, Jacques Prévert, Henry Miller, and, above all, Breton, Éluard and Aragon. He exhibited for the first time in Barcelona in 1918. A year later he moved to Paris where he adhered to the cubist movement and then, in 1924, passed into the ranks of the surrealists. But it may not be possible to catalog Miró's art: Miró is

unmistakeable, his mark moves in absolute freedom. Giulio Carlo Argan, the famous Italian art historian, defined him as «the nightingale of modern painting». The artist always moved beyond the frontiers of the rational and the senses and created one of the richest and most fascinating languages of 20th-century art.

On June 10, 1975, Joan Miró made Barcelona the best of all possible gifts: this was the day that the Foundation which bears his name, a cultural center which has raised Catalonia to the highest levels of world art, was inaugurated — the Fundación Joan Miró, Centro de Estudios de Arte Contemporaneo». The building which houses the Foundation is on the hill of Montjuich and was built by Josep-Lluis Sert. The following year, a large exhibition of 475 drawings (covering the period 1901 to 1975) marked the formal inauguration. In 1978 the European Council awarded the Miró Foundation with the «Special Prize for a Museum», an international acknowledgment of the imaginative work of the Catalan painter. «What is closest to my heart is Catalonia and the dignity of man» are what the artist said.

*Montjuich: entrance to the old castle.*

# MONTJUICH

A speechless Don Quixote contemplated a battle between the Christian fleet and the Saracen fleet from these heights. A system of signals, quite sophisticated for the time (banners and bonfires), signalled the position of the enemy ships to the Catalan admirals from Montjuich. This hill, 213 meters high above the harbor of Barcelona, maintained this function until 1401.

The hill of Montjuich is one of the most interesting spots in the city. Laya, the ancient village of the Iberians who were the first inhabitants of Catalonia, rose here. The Romans built a road between the «Mons Taber» where their colony was situated and the hill which they may have called «Mons Jovis», Jupiter's Mountain. This was the first name of Montjuich, later rebaptized «Mons Judaicus», probably because it was the site of a Hebrew cemetery. Montjuich has always been a strategic link in the defenses of Barcelona, a key element in its system of lookouts and surveillance. In 1640, after the war «dels Segadors» against Philip IV, the city of Barcelona built a military fortification, the Citadel or Castle, on the top of Montjuich. When the city surrendered to Philip V's Bourbon armies at the end of the unfortunate War of Succession to the Spanish throne, the Castle was transformed into a military prison. Not until the early 60s, did the army turn the old Castle over to the city. Barcelona installed a *Museum of Military History* there, with antique weapons, mementos of the battle of Lepanto, relics of Catalan and Arab history and whole armies of lead soldiers. A marvelous panorama of Barcelona can be had from the bastions of the Castle.

The hill of Montjuich which surrounds the Citadel is a real spectacle: gardens, monuments, an amusement park, museums and palaces make it an irresistable attraction for tourists and Barcelonians. Montjuich owes its present splendor to the intuition of the architect Amargós and the French landscape architect Forestier and the work done to prepare for the 1929 Exposition. Along its avenues are the Palacio Nacional, built expressly for the Fair, the Pabellón de la Rosaleda which houses the *Ethnological Museum*, the *Archaeological Museum*, a Greek theater, the botanical gardens, the *Font del Gat*, the reconstruction of the Pueblo Español, the *Fundación Joan Miró* and the *Miramar*, which dominates all of Barcelona.

Montjuich: the funicular.

Montjuich: the monument to the Sardana.

# THE FUNICULAR
# OF MONTJUICH

The cableway which connects the maritime district of
Barceloneta to Montjuich is the most spectacular of the
various approaches to the hill which dominates the city.
It was made famous by Michelangelo Antonioni's film,
«Professione Reporter». Rising from the port of Barcelo-
na to the balcony of Miramar it touches two high metal
towers, the Tower of Saint Sebastian and the Tower of
Jaime I, from which the aerial trip over the harbor of
Barcelona can be begun.

# SARDANA

The choral dance of the Sardana is the expression of
the Catalan people. On the hill of Montjuich the sculptor José Cañas has placed his *monument to the Sardana*.
No Sunday passes but one comes across great circles of
people in the streets of Barcelona who, holding hands,
with a proud and vaguely aristocratic air, are dancing
the Sardana with its varied rhythms, calm or restless, of
ever more rapid short steps.

*Gran Vía de los Corts Catalanes.*

*Plaza de Toros Monumental:* ▶ *general view and details.*

# PLAZA DE TOROS

There are two large arenas in Barcelona where the famous «corridas» take place — the **Plaza de Toros Las Arenas** and the **Plaza de Toros Monumental**, situated along the Gran Vía de los Corts Catalanes. Built between 1913 and 1916, the latter can seat almost 20,000 spectators.

Even though it was built after Las Arenas (which dates to 1900) the Monumental is particularly prestigious, quite in keeping with the outstanding role Barcelona has achieved in the field of «corridas» throughout Spain. Every year more than 200 bulls are killed in the arenas of this city. Bull fighting, which was already known to ancient Greece and Rome, was practiced in Spain as early as the second century. Traditionally each corrida requires six bulls over four years old, and three «matadores», who each kill two bulls drawn by lot, with the help of three «cuadrillas», each of which consists of five or six men.

The other figures who take part in this picturesque spectacle include: the «peones» or «banderilleros» who provoke the bull to arouse him, using the cape, and the «picadores» on horseback, who repeatedly strike him with the «puya» to weaken him. When the trumpet finally announces the «tercio de muerte», the last of the three stages into which the spectacle is divided, it is the turn of the «matador» or «espada», who exhibits himself in a series of figures and dangerous passages before killing the animal using a «muleta» (the red cape kept taut by a stick), quickly replacing the stick with a razor sharp sword with which to deal the fatal blow.

The bull, who drops dead in his tracks, is dragged out of the arena by gayly caparisoned horses, accompanied by the enthusiastic cheers of the crowd, which only a few seconds before (the final phase never lasts more than a quarter of an hour) was completely carried away by the exciting contemplation of the life and death struggle which has always fascinated, repelled and deeply moved man.

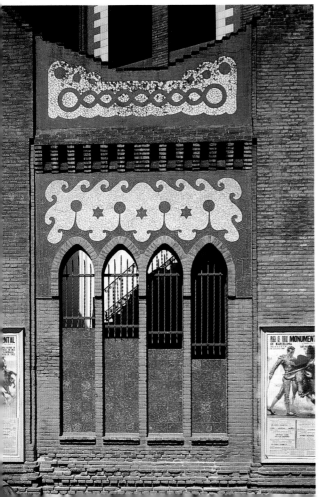

# ANTONIO GAUDÍ AND BARCELONA

Antonio Gaudí is one of the oustanding figures in modern art, «the» builder of 1900, as defined by Le Corbusier in 1957. Gaudí was born on June 25th, 1852 to a humble family of iron workers near Tarragona. The two neighboring cities of Reus and Riusdoms both vied for the honor of being his birthplace. In any case, Gaudí's early school years were spent in Reus, at the school of Francisco Berenguer, the father of one of his future assistants. In 1869 Gaudí arrived in Barcelona where he attended the University. His extraordinary capacities and his outstanding personal qualities came to the fore at once, characterized by his attention to detail and a particular enthusiasm for decoration, especially in wrought iron. Tangible evidence is to be found in the *two lamps* on the Plaza Real, their bases decorated with the coats of arms of Barcelona and crowned by the winged helmet of Mercury, symbol of the city's commercial interests. Is is quite likely that Gaudí collaborated on the designs for the Parque de la Ciudadela even before leaving the University, which he was to terminate in 1878. The four splendid winged dragons on the front of the waterfall may be by him. He greatly admired the work of Viollet-Le-Duc. During one of his rare journeys, Gaudí arrived in Carcassone just when the French architect was in the process of restoring the walls of the fortress. The Spanish architect was so intent in studying this work that the citizens of Carcasonne mistook him for the French master. Despite the bottomless pit which separated the two architects — Viollet-Le-Duce agnostic and experimentalist of new techniques and Gaudí a believer and traditionalist in his work — many aspects of their personalities were reciprocally assimilated. Even so, Gaudí elaborated an extremely personal style of his own that was so unique that it left its mark on the whole city, giving it an unmistakable character and distinguishing it from all other Spanish cities.

The extraordinary relationship between Gaudí and Barcelona was however to be brusquely interrupted. On June 7th, 1926, Gaudí was hit by a tram as he was leaving the work yard of the Sagrada Familia. None of the passersby recognized him and he was taken to the hospital of the poor where he died three days later. His mortal remains now rest in the crypt of the cathedral.

Mention has already been made of the fact that Gaudí immediately left his mark on the city of Barcelona. His first truly important work was *Casa Vicens*, commissioned in 1878 but begun in 1883. Since the site, the tranquil and simple calle Carolinas, is extremely narrow, Gaudí decided to stress the height of the building by running the chimneys down the facade. While he was working on Casa Vicens, Gaudí began on another commission. In 1884, the rich cotton industrialist Eusebio Güell commissioned two pavilions for his summer residence in Pedralbes, in the outskirts of Barcelona. The two *Güell Pavilions*, on the corner of what is now avenida de la Victoria, one octagonal and

the other rectangular, are united by a splendid wrought-iron gate in the form of a dragon. Between 1885 and 1890 Gaudí built the *palace* facing the calle del Asalto, again for Eusebio Güell who «discovered» him in the Paris Wold Fair in 1878. For the first time Gaudí turned his attention to the play of space on the roof, covering the chimneys and the aeration system with pieces of tile, and arranging them around the central cone which corresponds to the internal dome and through the openings of which the light penetrates and spreads throughout the building. The interior is a magnificent synthesis of ivory and marble, carved wood, frosted glass, and gilt metal.

A completely different spirit — formal simplicity and aesthetic rigor — pervades the *Convent and School of Saint Teresa*, begun in 1889. The year before, Gaudí had begun work on the *Casa Calvet*, commissioned by the textile manufacturer Pedro Martin Calvet, and for which he had even won a prize from the municipal authorities. Gaudí's imagination went wild inside in the realization of the elevator which has been transformed into a complicated reliquary in carved wood and wrought iron, surrounded by an elaborate baldachin supported on twisted granite columns which continue along the entire height of the building. The *villa of «Bellesguard»*, on the Tibidabo, also dates back to more or less the same period. It is characterized above all by the shape of the roof, a truncated pyramid pierced by projecting dormers at the corners.

*Portrait of Antonio Gaudí.*

Parque Güell: the imaginative pavilions
at the entrance to the park.

# PARQUE GÜELL

From 1900 onwards, with Eusebio Güell as his patronance more, Gaudí created one of his loveliest works, *Parque Güell*. The genius and art of the Spanish architect could never have been expressed as it was without the presence of his patron, Eusebio Güell y Bacigalupi, in Barcelona. The wealthy count of Güell, who greatly admired the English garden-cities so fashionable at the time, wanted to create a residential district of about 60 homes on 15 hectares of land he owned in a zone called «Montaña Pelada». The inhabitants were promised a new revolutionary way of life. Gaudí was commissioned to prepare an ideal town plan, with complete freedom of expression as far as buildings and ornaments were concerned. Despite the most optimistic previsions, the experiment of the new garden-city failed. Only two of the 60 plots were sold, one to Gaudí himself and the other to a friend, Dr. Alfonso Trias. That is why in 1922 the city of Barcelona acquired the entire area and transformed it into a public park. A high encircling wall encloses the park. The main entrance is at the intersection with via Olot. The two curious pavilions in polychrome tile which flank the splendid wrought-iron gate were originally meant to serve as a porter's lodge (the one on the right) and as administration headquarters (on the left). A double staircase departs from the entrance and the flights of stairs, united

by ornamental waterworks and zoomorphic sculptures covered with mosaics (including dragons which are always present in Gaudí's art) meet at the top in what is commonly called the «room of the hundred columns», even if there are really only 86. In this capricious «hypostyle hall» the columns in Doric style bend to support a vault which also seems to be moving because it is wavy, and, in unexpected anticipation of Pop Art, encrusted with pieces of bottles, plates, glass and ceramics. In 1912 Gaudí put the crowning touch on this room in what is considered the symbol and synthesis of his «total art», that is the great curved bench which marks the boundaries of the upper terrace overlooking the city. It is said that in his attempt to give the bench seat an anatomical form, Gaudí had one of his workers sit nude on the wet plaster and thus obtained the profile which he then used in designing the seat. Here too, Gaudí is once more a skilled forerunner of the form and color of an art which was yet to come: in fact the entire bench is composed of a mosaic of ceramic shards of various colors and sizes which he arranged in a gigantic abstract collage.

At the center of the park is Gaudí's unusual house-museum, where he lived from 1906 to 1926 and which still preserves the furniture, paintings, and objects which belonged to the great Catalan artist.

Parque Güell: the entrance staircase
to the Hall of the Hundred Columns.

Parque Güell: an odd fountain.

Parque Güell: the name of the park as
it can be seen at the entrance.

*Parque Güell: the Hall of the Hundred Columns seen from the top of the staircase.*

*Parque Güell: the Hall of the Hundred Columns with the so-called Gran Plaza above.*

*Parque Güell: museum in Gaudí's home.*

## CASA BATLLÓ

Casa Batlló, at no. 43 Paseo de Gracia, rose between 1904 and 1906 in the city block known as the «manzana de la discordia» or the «Apple of Discord», with its diverse examples of Catalan modernist architecture standing side by side. Since manzana means both apple and city block, this is also a play on words. Casa Batlló was restored by Gaudí for the family of José Batlló y Casanovas. Gaudí applied his own extremely personal style to the whole building, restructuring the facade, restoring the interior and redesigning the furniture. An «immense, senseless multicolor mosaic shimmering with scintillating light from which forms of water emerge» is what Salvador Dalí had to say of Casa Batlló. The cult of the curved line and the expansion of the form as a pure vital symbol, reach their apex here: everything, from the columns to the balconies, is seen as something that must be made to vibrate and live.

## CASA MILÁ

Casa Milá, begun in 1905 and finished five year later, also faces Paseo de Gracia. A glance at the facade suffices to explain why this five-story building is better known as «La Pedrera» or the quarry.

The Pedrera may very well be the best and most complete example of Gaudí's concept of Nature: a sort of stone mountain created by man, with a group of «caverns» which open onto the facade which emanates an enormous vital force.

Gaudí, this solitary introvert and fervent Catholic, succeeded here in transforming the most profound moment of Art Nouveau into an expression of pure vitality: something that is no longer a static geometric space, but a space which expands with its birth and development. The facade thus materializes in a series of waves which follow the movement of the entire building. On the other hand, Gaudí himself once said: «...corners will disappear and the material will abundantly manifest itself in its astral rotondities: the sun will penetrate on all four sides and it will be the image of paradise... and my palace will be more luminous than light.»

But let us climb for a moment to the roof of the house, and receive the impact of the unrestrained fantasy of the artist. No railings, gardens overlooking deep courtyards and hooded monsters of an enigmatic and disquieting aspect. In this abstract stage-set (the bizarre shapes of the chimneys alone suffice) Gaudí anticipates by a good forty years the aspects of the best of surrealism.

# SAGRADA FAMILIA

Gaudí's intense series of works culminates in what is considered his masterpiece, even though it was left incomplete when he suddenly died — the *Sagrada Familia*.

In 1866, the book dealer Boca-

bella founded a spiritual association dedicated to St. Joseph. In 1881 two hectares of land in the Barrio del Poblet, a modest district in the outskirts of the city, were acquired with the contributions of a public subscription. Initially the construction of a church dedicated to the holy family was entrusted to the architects Martorell and Francesco del Villar. After having begun the construction of the crypt, the latter resigned and Martorell called in Gaudí who was then 31. On the death of the bookseller Bocabella, the Bishop of Barcelona officially took over what had been a private firm and formally put Gaudí in charge of the works. At the time, Gaudí had already finished the vault of the crypt and radically changed Villar's original plan. Gaudí saw the Sagrada Familia as a great symbolic building, a colossal allegory which was to evolve on the three monumental facades. The west facade was to be dedicated to the Birth of Christ, the one on the east to His life and the Passion, and the facade to the south to the Ascension. Of these three facades, Gaudí succeeded in realizing only the one to the west, which is so perfect and complete that it can be considered as a building in its own right. The three portals, which symbolize faith, hope, and charity, are completely covered with sculpture in Art Nouveau style, and the architecture disappears under a forest of vibrant figures which stretch, twist, and expand. The portal of Hope, dedicated to the Virgin, shows the mystical marriage between Mary and Joseph, the flight to Egypt and the massacre of the Innocents. The palm-shaped column is supported by a Nile tortoise, symbol of perseverance. The central portal of Charity is divided by the tree of descendants from Abraham to Joseph and is dominated by the grotto of Bethlehem. The cypress is

crowned by a tau cross and features a pelican, symbol of sacrifice, at its base. The last portal, on the right, is dedicated to St. Joseph and illustrates stories of Jesus in the Temple and carpenter's whorkshop.

A glimpse of Gaudí's working methods throws some light on the composition of the allegoric representations. The master used to choose his models off the street, then photograph them against a set of mirrors so as to have a complete view from all angles. After that he made a plaster cast which he then used for the figure, modifying the proportions as he saw fit. It is truly a pity that this extraordinary neo-Gothic building was never finished. The models preserved in the crypt show Barcelona's «unfinished cathedral» as a traditional Latin cross plan, with five aisles crossing a transept that is three aisles wide. The nave is illuminated by wide windows and was to have been a real forest of columns, each dedicated to a saint, an apostle, or a bishop. At the crossing, a colossal central tower, the symbol of Christ, was to rise up surrounded by four smaller towers (sym-

bols of the Four Evangelists). Each of the three facades was to have four bell towers, making a total of twelve, to symbolize the Apostles.

This enormous complex vision, with its emphasiv on the vertical so as to symbolize the union of sky and earth, was to be further completed by brilliant colours, as is evident from the model which Gaudí presented to the 1910 Paris Exposition. On the Nativity facade, the portal of Hope was to have been green, symbolizing the valley of the Nile. The portal of Charity was to be the blue of a night in Bethlehem and the portal of Faith was to have been burnt Sienna to symbolize the sands of Palestine. The interior of the church was also to have been colored: white and gold in the right aisle to sym-

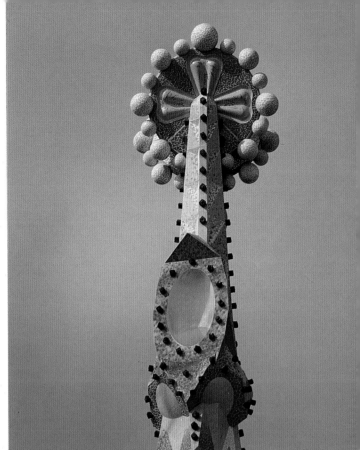

*Sagrada Familia: spires seen from below.*

bolize joy, violet and black in the left side aisle to symbolize grief.

Gaudí threw himself heart and soul into this colossal work. In 1914 when he was already 62 he even decided to live in a room in the building yard of the church. When he died, the work was carried on, according to his plans by a group of his closest collaborators including Sugranes, Quintana and Matamela. Work was interrupted in 1935 when the Spanish Civil War broke out, during which time a fire destroyed part of the building and many plans and models in Gaudí's studio. Ever today, financed by the offerings of the faithful, construction continues, albeit extremely slowly. When it is finished the church should be 110 meters long and 45 meters high — one of the largest and finest churches in the Christian world.

Sagrada Familia: crypt.

One of the museum rooms documenting
the construction of the Sagrada Familia.

Sagrada Familia: Coronation of
the Virgin on the so-called
Nativity facade.

# BARCELONA'S SURROUNDINGS

## PALACIO NACIONAL DE PEDRALBES

Pedralbes is one of the wealthiest residential districts in the city, where Art Nouveau buildings sit side by side with elegant villas and dignified constructions of more recent date. In any case the green of the hedges and gardens is the predominating note.

The Palacio Nacional de Pedralbes is in the University City, near the end of the Diagonal, and was built between 1919 and 1929 as a residence for the heads of state or other important visitors. It is open to the public and surrounded by an enchanting park which also shelters an interesting *Coach Museum*.

A guided visit allows us to admire the rich decoration of the interiors (outstanding is the sumptuous *Throne room*, with its vault entirely covered with painted architecture), the furnishings, in part from Italy, and the valuable collections of porcelains, clocks, tapestries, fans and paintings (some by Luca Giordano), which are periodically renewed.

*Palacio Nacional de Pedralbes: bedroom.* ▶

*Palacio Nacional de Pedralbes: the facade on the garden.*

*Palacio Nacional de Pedralbes: the study.* ▶

*Palacio Nacional de Pedralbes:
two views of the sumptuous throne room.*

*Real Monasterio de Pedralbes: exterior.* ▶

*Real Monasterio de Pedralbes: cloister.* ▶

# REAL MONASTERIO DE PEDRALBES

This monastery, one of the most suggestive signs of ancient Barcelona, was founded by Queen Elisenda de Montcada, fourth and last wife of Jaime II. Designed by Guillem d'Abiell, it was built between 1326 and 1419 by Ferrer Peiró and by Domenech Granyena and is one of the finest extant examples of Catalan Gothic. Only part of the monastery is open to the public for it is at present lived in by the nuns of Saint Claire.

Noteworthy on the exterior of the church is the fine octagonal tower and, on the facade, the emblems of the Montcada family. Inside, the single majestic nave with 14th century stained-glass windows contains the monumental *tomb of Queen Elisenda*.

The *Chapter House* is also fine, ornamented with a stained-glass window from the first half of the 15th century. The airy cloister, with three superposed orders of galleries supported by elegant small columns, leads to the *chapel of San Miguel*, with its splendid frescoes of the *Stories of the Life of the Virgin*, by Ferrer Bassa (1290-1348), one of the greatest Catalan painters and illuminators of the 14th century. Active also for some years in Italy, Bassa has endowed the ecstatic figurines in the various scenes, dominated by a uniform blue ground, with various elements that come from contemporary Sienese and Giottesque painting. Dating to 1343, the paintings are well preserved.

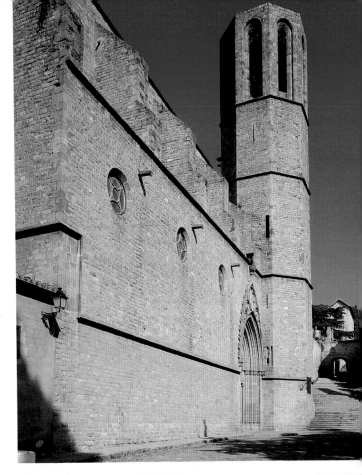

*Tibidabo: two views of the Amusement Park.*

*Tibidabo: the church of the Sacred Heart.* ▶

# TIBIDABO

The Tibidabo is the highest summit (over 500 meters) of Collcerola, or better of the hills surrounding the city and protecting it from the winds of the north.

An overall panorama can be had from this modest crest, which can be reached by bus or cable car or by car. It includes the entire city with the ocean in the background, the other summits of the chain (such as «La Rabassada» and «San Pedro Mártir»), as well as Montserrat, and beyond, the Pyrenean summits.

Halfway down its green slopes is the **Astronomical Observatory** and the *Museum of Physical Sciences*, which were created early in the 20th century thanks to Camillo Fabra, marquis of Allella.

The crest of Tibidabo is crowned by the majestic church of the Sacred Heart, built in Gothic style by the architect Enrique Sagnier. An elevator inside the church further amplifies the already vast panorama offered by Tibidabo. On the highest spire of the building a *statue of Jesus* with widespread arms seems to lean out over the underlying city. Tibidabo is a favorite goal for tourists and natives, with an **Amusement Park** as one of its attractions. Surrounded by terraces, avenues, large squares, and charming gardens, the roller coaster, the labyrinth, the haunted house, various meeting places and characteristic bars and restaurants create an ideal atmosphere for relaxation and entertainment.

Montserrat: the monastery
and the apse of the church.

Montserrat: general view of the monastery.

Montserrat: the interior of the church.

# MONTSERRAT

The mountain of Montserrat rises about 30 kilometers north of Barcelona. Its highest summit, known as S. Girolamo, is over a thousand meters high. The Catalan term «Montserrat», or serrated mountain, is a good name for the aspect of this massive ridge, with the stony conglomerate, prevalently sandstone, which erosion has modelled into extremely suggestive strange silhouettes and forms, to which the fantasy of man has given various names (the giant, the camel, cat's head, bell, etc.).

The wealth and variety of the local flora is also surprising. The goal of many trekkers, Montserrat also attracts many enthusiastic tourists.

As far back as the 8th century various unidentified hermitages existed on Montserrat. In later times these included the hermitage of S. María, converted by Bishop Oliva in the 11th century into a small monastery, the forerunner of the present sanctuary, which was to become famous throughout Catalonia thanks to the image of the miraculous Romanesque Madonna (12th century) still in the sanctuary today and called «Moreneta» by the Catalans for the dark color of her skin. According to legend she appeared in a cave in the mountain.

The monastery soon became known all over Europe, and religious buildings dedicated to the Madonna of Montserrat rose everywhere. Thanks to the hermit Bernardo Boil, travelling companion of Christopher Columbus, the cult of the Madonna of Montserrat also reached the New World (an island in the Antilles received the name of Montserrat). Among the most famous personages connected with the monastery are Giuliano della Rovere (future Julius II), who was responsible for the building of the cloister in Gothic style (1467), the Emperor Ferdinand III, who donated generously to the Benedictine community, Francesco Borgia, Luigi Gonzaga, Saint Ignatius of Loyola, Goethe and Schiller, who immortalized the mountain in some of their works.

From the 16th century on, the church, numerous annexes of the monastery, and buildings for the pilgrims, who increased as the place became more famous, were added to the original hermitage.

In 1811 the monastery was sacked by the Napoleonic army and the successive revolutionary uprisings reduced Montserrat to a pile of ruins abandoned by the monks.

*Montserrat: the St. Jerome in the museum.*

*Montserrat: the famous «Moreneta».*

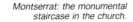

*Montserrat: the monumental staircase in the church.*

*Montserrat: a room in the museum.*

The rapid rebirth of the sanctuary which began in the middle of the 19th century continued despite the last civil war (1936-1939) thanks to the intervention of the autonomous government of Barcelona.

The present monastery rises on a narrow ledge about 700 meters high. The large basilica was built between 1559 and 1592 and is more than 60 meters long and over 30 meters high. The facade, as we see it today, dates to the 60s. The elegant **interior**, with a single nave scanned by Gothic arches and flanked by side chapels, ends in a richly decorated apse, which dates to the second half of the 19th century. From here a marble staircase leads to the chapel which houses the wooden polychrome statue of the *Madonna of Montserrat* (patron saint of Catalonia ever since 1881). The Madonna and Child are seated on a throne decorated in gold and silver reliefs by famous Catalan artists: behind her is a finely storied retablo (1947).

Montserrat: the lovely Gothic cloister.

Montserrat: the monumental tomb
of Joan of Aragon.

Montserrat: suggestive
panoramas from the cable car.

Besides the *Escolanía* (the old school for the prepara-
tion of young choirboys), the large *library* (containing
over 200,000 volumes) and the old *typography*, founded
in the 15th century, the museum is particularly noteworthy. Its *picture gallery* contains among others, paintings by Berruguete, El Greco, Zurbarán, Velvet
Brueghel, Mignard, Caravaggio and Guardi.

The *Chapel of Santa Cueva* can be reached by a path
or by cable car. It was built by Gaudí in the place on
which the Virgin appeared in 880.

San Juan also provides a fine view of the monastery,
while the *belvedere* near the chapel of San Jeronimo,
reached by cable car, offers a splendid panorama
which, when the weather is fine, arrives as far as the
Pyrenees.

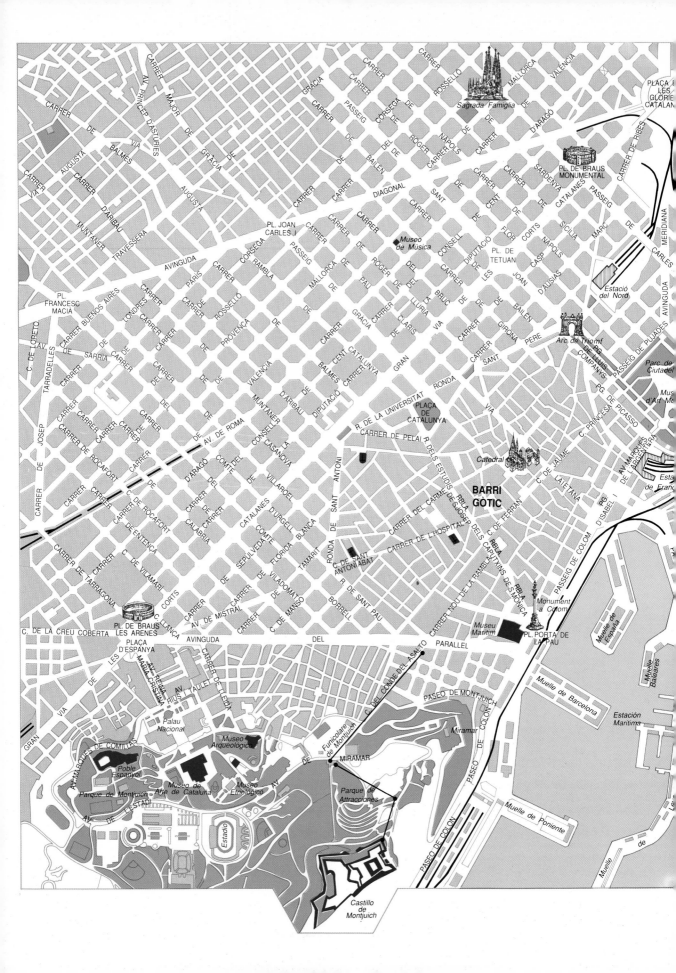